Original title:
Bubbles and Reflections

Copyright © 2025 Creative Arts Management OÜ
All rights reserved.

Author: Isaac Ravenscroft
ISBN HARDBACK: 978-1-80587-277-1
ISBN PAPERBACK: 978-1-80587-747-9

Echoes in a Sphere

In a globular world, giggles float,
Round and round like a merry goat.
Chasing shadows, they bounce away,
Tickled by the light of day.

Laughter pops, like popcorn flies,
Silly whispers dance and rise.
A rainbow swirl, a jolly sight,
Who knew spheres could bring such light?

Floating Moments

Up in the air, a playful jest,
A helium heart in a feathery nest.
Valentine clouds, with smiles so wide,
Drifting dreams set off on a ride.

In the breeze, a cheeky wink,
Chortles and chuckles make us think.
Life's a tease, a fragile chase,
With colors swirling, a merry embrace.

Fragile Glass Serenade

A crystal ball rolls down the street,
Twirling giggles, oh so sweet.
Shattered dreams of laughter bright,
Juggling joy with all its might.

Dancing shadows in the sun,
Each twirl whispers, 'Let's have fun!'
Glassy echoes, a clumsy song,
Where silly moments all belong.

Dance of the Orb

Round and round, the mischief spins,
Jumpy leaps, and goofy grins.
Orbs are rolling, feet in flight,
Twisting tales from morning light.

Floating high with silly flair,
Chasing giggles everywhere.
In this merry, spinny race,
Laughter paints the happy space.

Floating Thoughts in Stillness

In a glass of water, dreams do spin,
Skimming on laughter, where thoughts begin.
A light-hearted dance of whimsical sights,
As giggles and wishes float on delights.

Marbles beneath, they play hide and seek,
Silly and joyful, this moment unique.
With a splash of humor, they shimmer and glow,
Echoes of joy in the currents below.

Chasing Rainbow Illusions

A chase through the air, colors fly high,
Tickling the clouds, where whimsy does lie.
Chasing a shimmer that teases the eye,
A wink from the sun, as laughter sails by.

Prancing on shadows that giggle with glee,
Each twist and turn, a joyful decree.
With points of bright laughter, they wink and they jest,
In a carnival dance, we're all at our best.

The Luminous Dancer

In puddles of light, a figure does twirl,
Underneath the sun, where bright ripples swirl.
With every spin, droplets leap in delight,
A fanciful show that sparks day and night.

Her laughter a melody, soft as a breeze,
Floating in rhythm, she dances with ease.
Each shimmer a tickle, a playful retreat,
As joy leaps around, isn't life rather sweet?

Celestial Ripples

Stars dip and swirl in a cosmic embrace,
Making the sky a giggling place.
With giggles and jiggles, they leap through the night,
Moonbeams chortle, a whimsical sight.

Chasing their shadows, they play tag with the sun,
Illusions so goofy, it's all just for fun.
In the cosmos, we find a mirthful array,
Funny little glimmers, leading us astray.

A Symphony of Droplets

In the park, they dance with glee,
Popping here and there, they flee.
A chubby kid with sticky hands,
Chasing dreams like silly bands.

Laughter spills like fizzy soda,
A splashy tune, oh what a moda!
With every burst, the giggles rise,
Like tiny fireworks in sunny skies.

Kaleidoscope of Moments

Colors swirl, a dizzy run,
Each twist and turn brings out the fun.
A cat leaps up, then takes a dive,
In this whirl, we feel alive!

Shiny spots catch playful eyes,
As children laugh and never sighs.
A parade of smiles, unlimited cheer,
In this wild world, joy is near.

Reflections in the Current

In the puddles, shadows play,
Wobbly forms dance and sway.
A frog wears glasses, quite absurd,
Croaking tunes, he's truly stirred!

While ducks quack in their own tune,
A wiggly worm hums to the moon.
Splashes echo with a silly beat,
Nature's joke is quite the treat!

Glimmering Echoes

Shiny orbs hover in the sun,
Reflecting laughs, oh what fun!
A dog races, slips on a leaf,
Chasing light like a comic thief.

These sparkly friends, so bold and bright,
Ask us to play from morning till night.
Join the chase, don't miss the cheer,
For silliness lives when smiles are near.

Glimmering Contemplations

In a soda can, thoughts do dance,
Fizzing up dreams, given the chance.
Lost in a pop, a sweet serenade,
Bouncing like merriment, they've got it made.

Thoughts float like confetti, high and bright,
A carnival glance in the sparkling light.
Laughter swells, they tumble and sway,
In fizzy exchanges, we giggle away.

The Light's Embrace

In a sunny room where giggles dwell,
Shadows twist and turn, like stories to tell.
A flicker here, a shimmer there,
Whispers of glee linger in the air.

Every glint a jest, sending us into fits,
As laughter bounces off these playful bits.
The sun, a joker, throws light on our play,
In radiant grins, we brighten the day.

Veils of Imagination

Behind a curtain of playful haze,
Ideas swirl in a mischievous daze.
Colors collide, a rainbow's delight,
Laughter erupts in this whimsical sight.

Each thought a jester, twirling with cheer,
Tickling the senses, bringing us near.
A canvas of giggles painted so bold,
A tapestry of joy, a sight to behold.

Across the Undulating Surface

On a wobbly path where winks are found,
Giggles ripple out, creating a sound.
With each tiny wave, a chuckle ignites,
A splash of delight in playful sights.

Zooming along on a bouncy spree,
Each curve a giggle, just wait and see.
With every dip, a chorus of cheer,
Rolling in laughter, we hold it dear.

Liquid Mirages

In a glass of soda, a dance so sweet,
A fizzy high-jump, a bubbly beat.
Sipping too fast, I see stars in the sky,
Did I just burp, or did my dreams fly?

A spoon in my ice cream, a life's test drive,
Look! A frosty laugh, it's alive, oh my!
Chasing the patterns, they swirl and twirl,
Forgot my spoon; my face does a whirl.

Shimmering Fantasies

In a glassy pond, the ducks wear crowns,
Waddling in circles, like royalty clowns.
A splash from the side, oh no—what a scene!
The king turns to see if his court's still clean.

With each little ripple, the laughter grows loud,
Splashes of water draw in a crowd.
I joined in the fun, made the silliest sound,
Now I'm the wettest jester around.

The Hushed Surface

The pond looks so calm, a mirror in disguise,
I tiptoe on the edge; oh, what a surprise!
A leap and a splash, my friends giggle and shriek,
Turns out the water prefers a little sneak!

The dragonflies shimmer, having tea, oh so posh,
While I fumble my footing—splash! Splash! Oh gosh!
They zoom with a giggle, I'm left in a bind,
In this watery world, I swear the fish mind.

Dreams in a Crystal Pool

The shallow end whispers secrets of fun,
Where rubber ducks float under the sun.
I dive for treasure, but what do I find?
A lost flip-flop and memories entwined.

Sunbeams bounce merrily off each shiny wave,
I'm a mermaid princess, oh yes, I'm so brave!
With a splash and a laugh, I swim to the shore,
Leaving behind tales of soft water lore.

Chasing the Unseen

A wobbly dance upon the sea,
With squiggly lines that want to flee.
Chasing shadows, oh what a spree,
While seagulls cackle and sip their tea.

I chased a phantom, it slipped away,
"Did you see that?" I shouted in play.
It giggled back in a gleeful sway,
And rolled on the waves like a game of clay.

Celestial Waters

In a puddle, the stars dip low,
They swim in rings with an awkward flow.
I tried to catch one, my hands all aglow,
But it splashed my face, oh the cosmic show!

A fish in a bowtie gave me a wink,
As I tumbled about, missing the link.
The moon went mad, it began to blink,
While I pondered on how to rethink.

The Rippled Mirror

A pond that giggles at a passing breeze,
Reflecting laughter with winkles of tease.
The frogs are jesters, all hopping with ease,
While dragons fly by, causing such wheeze!

I tossed a stone to stir up the charm,
And in reply, the waters disarm.
With each little plop, I felt a warm calm,
As the ripples danced, sweet and warm.

Tornado of Colors

A whirlwind spins in a carnival glow,
Painting the skies with a vibrant show.
Its laughter erupts like a wild taco,
While the world below spins fast, don't you know?

Confetti of joy fills the air with a thrill,
As kittens ride rainbows for a big thrill.
The chortling clouds, oh what a skill,
Leave us all dizzy, our hearts happily fill.

Moonlight on a Still Pool

Twinkle toes of silvery glow,
Dance on water, moving slow.
Frogs in tuxedos leap with glee,
While fish wear hats and sip their tea.

The ducks compose a croaky tune,
Waltzing with the lazy moon.
Splashing popcorn, giggling fish,
Prancing graze on salsa swish.

While crickets chirp their happy sound,
And dragonflies whirl all around,
Each ripple tells a silly tale,
As night unveils its quirky trail.

Dreams Riding the Surface

Thoughts like clouds in pastel shades,
Float and drift in bright parades.
Laughter bounces from the shore,
As daydreams dance and wish for more.

A rubber duck with glasses on,
Pretends he's wise, a sage anon.
He quacks profound philosophy,
While swans roll eyes sarcastically.

Tiny boats with sailors bold,
Trade their tales of treasure gold.
But jellyfish just laugh so sweet,
As seaweed serves them bubble tea.

Pressed Against the Sky

In a puddle, the world is wide,
A giddy place where dreams can ride.
Acorns giggle, squirrels cheer,
While flipping coins makes wishes clear.

Here comes a cloud, all dressed in white,
Ready to join the fun tonight.
It slips and slides, a playful tease,
Mimicking shapes among the trees.

While ants parade with tiny drums,
And fireflies flash their buzzing hums,
Each glimmer cast in evening's glow,
Turns mundane things to quite the show.

Enchanted Reflections

Mirrors dance upon the ground,
Echoes of laughter swirl around.
A cat in shades sips lemonade,
While shadows join the masquerade.

Goldfish in tuxes trade their pearls,
With wispy dreams of giggling swirls.
Together they start a flash mob,
While to the rhythm, frogs all sob.

The evening shapes a jaunty scene,
Where every crack is quite the queen.
A slice of moon bites on the cheek,
As night ignites a playful peek.

Drifting Essence

In the air they dance with glee,
Round and shiny, such a spree.
Little giggles, pop and swirl,
They float along like dreams unfurl.

Chasing sunlight, a playful game,
Each one unique, none the same.
They rise and fall; what a sight!
Tickling the breeze, pure delight!

Glimmers of joy in the sky,
With every puff, they float and sigh.
Mischievous wisps of laughter's song,
In their tender bubble throng.

Oh dear friend, don't let them burst,
For in their presence, joy is first.
A fleeting joke, a nod to cheer,
These wispy wonders bring us near.

Prism of Solitude

A lonely sphere upon the floor,
Reflecting joys from days of yore.
It rolls and wobbles, oh so round,
In its clear world, silence found.

Twirling shadows, playful mime,
Whispering secrets of the time.
A smile dances, bright yet shy,
As quirky patterns flutter by.

Up on high, it glistens bright,
A tiny sun in fading light.
With every sway and tiny hop,
A giggling jest, it can't be stopped!

Lonely yet buoyant, full of cheer,
An odd little friend, it holds us near.
Laughter echoes, unique and true,
In its colorful prism view.

Floating in Time

Drifting lightly through the air,
A comical twist, without a care.
Tickled by whispers and winds they roam,
Each a traveler far from home.

Hitching rides on passing dreams,
Dancing lightly on sunlight beams.
They joke and jostle, round and round,
In the sky, pure joy is found.

Swirling moments, no need to rush,
Twisting, turning in a playful hush.
They laugh at clocks, such funny fools,
For in their world, there are no rules.

A tickle here, a giggle there,
As time unwinds, with bubbles rare.
Floating whimsies, free and light,
In laughter's grasp, they take their flight.

The Blushing Horizon

A rosy glow at day's retreat,
Dipping low, it's quite the feat.
Silly tones of orange and pink,
Painting the sky, time to think.

Laughter spills from clouds so bright,
A cheeky wink in fading light.
Horizon blushes, a shy affair,
As twinkling stars start to glare.

With every sunset comes the fun,
Dancing shadows, night begun.
Whimsical giggles, they float about,
Chasing giggles into the doubt.

Oh, the tales the sky could tell,
Of laughter heard and joy to dwell.
As day gives way to night's embrace,
The horizon grins, a happy face.

Liquid Laughter

In the glass, a giggle floats,
Wobbling like a jolly boat.
Frothy dreams bob up and down,
Wearing silly, fizzy crowns.

A splash of joy, a fizzing tune,
Each sip a chuckle, bright as noon.
Gulp it down, but maybe slow,
Or risk a squirt—a bubbly show!

Tickling tongues and silly grins,
Ticking clocks as laughter spins.
Every sip, a playful cheer,
In this fizzy atmosphere!

From fizzy sips to burpy trails,
Let's craft hilarity, it never fails.
Raise your glass, let laughter pour,
Cheers to joy, forevermore!

Serene Skies above

In fluffy clouds, the day does play,
With puffy smiles, it lights the way.
Chasing shadows, a whimsical race,
Cotton candy dreams embrace.

A giggle here, a chuckle there,
As silly geese honk in the air.
The sun gets tickled, bright and bold,
It laughs out loud, a sight to behold.

Each ray a grin, each breeze a tease,
Whispering secrets through the trees.
Yet in this calm, the laughter flies,
Drawing giggles from the skies!

The stars will wink when night is nigh,
And moonbeams dance as dreams float by.
So sit beneath this joyous dome,
With hearts alight, we find our home.

Journey Through the Glimmer

Wandering paths of sparkling light,
Where every shimmer feels just right.
With each step, a joyous jig,
As giggles dance, both sly and big.

The grass tickles as I glide,
With twinkling fairies by my side.
A whirling twist, a playful race,
Through glistening meadows, we find our place.

The sunshine winks, a playful tease,
As we roll 'round with giggling ease.
In this realm, hilarity blooms,
In every corner, laughter looms.

So take my hand, let's spin and sway,
In this bright land, we'll laugh and play.
For every glimmer hides a jest,
Come join the fun, let's be our best!

Shattered Illusions

A mirror cracked, a funny sight,
With silly faces, oh what a fright!
A jester's laugh in every shard,
Reflecting glee, a whimsical guard.

Each broken piece, a fleeting grin,
A gaudy dance where chaos begins.
Find the humor in every chip,
Let's topple giggles from this trip!

The world can spin, let's take a chance,
And tumble through this wild dance.
Flip the norm, let's raise a cheer,
For in the madness, joy is near!

So gather round this fractured light,
And laugh away into the night.
Through shattered dreams, we'll weave our fun,
For every mishap makes us one!

Surfaces that Sing

On a pond where the frogs leap,
The water giggles, oh so deep.
A wink from a lily with glee,
Tells secrets to fish, just wait and see.

The sky throws a fit, looking grand,
As clouds parade, a fluffy band.
Shimmering shapes dance on the shore,
They tickle the toes, then ask for more.

With splashes and plops, laughter erupts,
The playful goldfish, in fun, disrupts.
In ripples and waves, all is afloat,
Even old turtles, they chuckle and gloat.

Catch the light with a cheeky grin,
Nature's whimsy invites us in.
Join the fun; take a playful swing,
For here at the edge, we let our hearts sing.

Silken Reflections

In puddles where giggles reside,
Dancing raindrops take a ride.
They leap and twirl with a splash,
Painting the world with a bright, bold flash.

The mirror pond acts so coy,
Reflecting the antics of every girl and boy.
A splash from a pebble, oh what a sight,
Turns serious faces into pure delight.

Sunbeams wink on a froggy throne,
While snails slowly creep, never alone.
They whisper in jest, with a chuckle so sly,
As the dragonflies dart, zipping by.

Time stretches out, it twists and bends,
In this realm where silliness transcends.
So come take a dance, prance on the floor,
Here, joy is the rhythm, who could ask for more?

Harmonies in the Mist

In the morning, where fog likes to tease,
The trees wear hats, swaying with ease.
A chorus of chirps fills the air,
As squirrels debate, should they stop and stare?

Misty whirlwinds play hide and seek,
With giggles of critters, we all dare peek.
Each twist of the air carries a tune,
Even the daisies dance to the moon.

A tumble of leaves joins the refrain,
Tickling the ground with their merry campaign.
It's a party for shadows, throwing a fit,
As joyous whispers and laughter do sit.

Come join the mess of this playful scene,
Where everything sparkles and sparkles mean.
With friends all around, let's take the dive,
In this joyful symphony, we truly thrive!

Quiet Wanderings

Stumbling across a shiny creek,
I saw a sunbeam sneaking a peek.
It nudged a pebble, giggling bright,
As it rolled and danced, what a silly sight!

Wandering souls took a quiet turn,
With whispers of laughter, the willow would learn.
It swayed to the rhythm of chattering stars,
Inviting the fireflies to come play guitars.

With every step, the ground softly hums,
A parade of mischief where wisdom succumbs.
In the quiet of nature, the colors collide,
Making giggles emerge from the silence inside.

So here's to the playful, the light-hearted chase,
Through magical woods, we find our own space.
In every still moment, a tickle we find,
That keeps and curls laughter inside of the mind.

The Gentle Drift

A floating orb of mischief, so light,
It dances and sways, a comical sight.
It pops with a giggle, not quite a boast,
A fleeting delight, a wobbly ghost.

It teases the breeze, swirling with cheer,
It tumbles and tumbles, then suddenly, here!
It lands on a nose, causing a laugh,
As we chase after joy, in this merry gaffe.

Each shimmered breath, a tiny surprise,
Joy painted softly in children's wide eyes.
Like giggling fairies in mid-air flight,
Chasing the silly in shimmering light.

And when it finally goes *POP!* with a cheer,
We gather its spirits, keep them near.
In laughter we linger, a sweet, fleeting gift,
As we sway with the whims of a gentle drift.

Luminous Past

In corners of memories, bright beads we find,
They twinkle like stars, with laughter entwined.
A pastel parade, of colors so sweet,
They jiggle and jump, underfoot, they greet.

With squeezy delight, they waddle about,
As echoes of giggles dissolve all doubt.
When swept by the wind, they trip and they glide,
A circus of whimsy, an unseen ride.

Each fizz of delight brings back days that we've known,
Where joy wore a crown in our hearts, brightly shone.
A dance of the past, with a wink and a grin,
As laughter returns, let the fun begin!

So here's to those moments, like rainbows in mist,
That bubble up fast, when they're not to be missed.
We'll carry the memories wherever we roam,
In laughter and light, we will always feel home.

Threads of Vapor

A wispy delight, a joke on the breeze,
It twists and it curls, with giggles to tease.
A tapestry woven in soft, silly tones,
Spinning round corners, like soft, silly drones.

Watch as it lingers, like thoughts in the air,
Floating like laughter, without a care.
Each twist tells a secret, each turn brings a grin,
A dance of the vapor, where humor creeps in.

In a world full of whim, it puffs and it sighs,
With clownish intentions and light-hearted lies.
The threads of our joy weave a fun, crazy tale,
As we skip through the moments, like boats without sail.

So let's raise a chuckle and dance in delight,
With wisps that remind us, the world's full of light.
In laughter's embrace, let our spirits soar high,
As we linger in mirth, beneath the blue sky.

Interwoven Gleams

In a quilt made of giggles, we stitch up the fun,
With patches of wishes and races to run.
A pitter-patter riddle, where light-hearted cheers,
Play tag with our memories, far from our fears.

Like glimmers of sunlight through curtains of rain,
Each flicker a whisper, where nonsense remains.
Vivid hues chasing in spirals of cheer,
Spinning together, we hold it all dear.

The colors collide in a mosaic of joy,
As we frolic through moments, just girl and boy.
In laughter we gather, like marbles set free,
As we weave through the day, life's patchwork, you see!

For in every line, a sparkle takes flight,
In the madness of joy, we sparkle so bright.
Each gleaming embrace, we twine ever tight,
As we dance through our stories, in mirth's soft light.

Heavenly Echoes

In the sky, a plop and pop,
Cheerful sounds that never stop.
Round and round they giggle free,
Floating whispers, come dance with me.

A frothy laugh, a bouncy cheer,
Tickling toes, they disappear.
Chasing trails of laughter bright,
In this game of silly flight.

Watch them swirl, a wiggly sight,
Juggling joy in golden light.
Here we bounce, we roll and slide,
Join the party, take a ride!

When the day starts to settle down,
Ribbit goblins in the crown.
Echoes giggle in the street,
Squishy fun, oh what a treat!

Mirth in Curved Glass

In a cup, a giggle glows,
Jolly jokes the liquid knows.
Mirror faces twist and cheer,
Sipping silly, drawing near.

Cracked up mugs, a snorted grin,
Pour in laughter, let the fun begin.
Every sip, a little feat,
Wiggling joy, life's a sweet treat.

Bubbles bounce in woozy dance,
Ticklish fizzes, take a chance!
Laughter drips from every edge,
Time to make a juicy pledge!

Join the crew with sprightly zest,
Chasing giggles, we're the best.
In the glass, our spirits soar,
Mirth and mayhem—always more!

Soliloquy of Light

Shadows play in a twirly way,
Brightened giggles end the day.
Every spark has tales to tell,
In the glow of a wishful spell.

Prancing beams weave through the air,
Winking stars, a cheeky flare.
Frolicking with the sounds around,
The cheeky glow knows how to clown.

Glitters frolic, they skip and hop,
Making mischief, ready to pop.
Chase the shimmer, let it lead,
In the light, we sow the seed.

Casting shadows on the floor,
Whimsical whispers want more.
Let this journey take its flight,
In the giggles of fleeting light!

Ethereal Travels

Traveling through the fizzy dream,
Whirlwinds dance in a twinkly stream.
Oh look! A flight of giggles wide,
In this realm, we all can glide.

Lollipop clouds up in the sky,
Wobbly wonders floating by.
Giggling winds, a constant tease,
We spin around with joyful ease.

Frothy waves of chuckling cheer,
Flickering pathways draw us near.
Up and down, we twist and sway,
In this whimsy, come what may!

Zany trails of frolic roam,
In this wonderland, we're home.
Laugh out loud, embrace the flight,
Ethereal travels in pure delight!

Melodies of a Still Surface

In the pond, a frog takes flight,
He leaps with grace, oh what a sight!
A splashy dance, a sudden plop,
The water sings, then calls to stop.

With tiny rings that stretch and sway,
A fish swims by to steal the play.
It wiggles, giggles, oh so spry,
And makes the dragonflies all sigh.

A beetle spins, a whimsical twirl,
While lily pads around him swirl.
Their laughter echoes, light and free,
As water glasses toast with glee.

So come and join this ribbit fest,
Where amphibians find their jest.
The pond's a stage, a wacky show,
As nature's giggles ebb and flow.

Stars Beneath the Surface

Beneath the waves, the wink of light,
Where fish play hide-and-seek at night.
A starfish yells, 'Come dance with me!'
As seaweed sways so carelessly.

A crab in shoes, oh what a sight,
Treads softly on the ocean's height.
He moonwalks past with such finesse,
While clams just laugh at his fine dress.

Sea turtles giggle, rolling round,
Their little shells make charming sounds.
While an octopus, quite the jester,
Waves all his arms, a true investor.

So dive right in, the splash is key,
The ocean's filled with mystery.
But watch your step; it's slippery fun,
Where laughter pops like bubbles, won!

Liquid Labyrinths

In a cup of tea, a swirl appears,
It plays with thoughts and stirs up cheers.
A spoon dives deep, a merry whirl,
Then jumps out quick, watch it twirl!

With every sip, emotions flood,
A tiny splash, a little thud.
The milk joins in, a creamy dance,
While sugar cubes hold a chance.

They tumble down in sweet delight,
And giggle as they start to fight.
'Join us now!' the teacup sings,
As laughter bubbles up with wings.

So grab your cup, let's make a scene,
Where flavors mix, and joy is seen.
In liquid paths that loop and bend,
Heartfelt chuckles never end.

Beyond the Clear Veil

There's a world behind the glassy shield,
Where toys and shoes lie unsealed.
A little ghost with a wink so sly
Waves at all who glance nearby.

Fish tickle toes, oh what a tease,
As they glide past with utmost ease.
An echo of laughter stirs the air,
In this place, joy is everywhere.

Reflections twist, they giggle loud,
While shadows play, an electric crowd.
Old rubber ducks join in the fun,
Bouncing happily, they've just begun.

So peek beyond that shiny frame,
Where silliness stays, and none feel blame.
In this world of sheer delight,
Where every glance brings pure delight.

Fragments of Infinite Possibilities

In a glass of fizz, a dance begins,
A merry jig, where laughter spins.
Tiny worlds float, all twist and twirl,
Sipping joy, cheers unfurl.

Each sip a mystery, each giggle a cheer,
What's just a drink? A treasure, my dear!
With every pop, a silly surprise,
Who knew soda could tease our eyes?

A whimsy ride, like riding a kite,
Gravity giggles, oh what a sight!
Drink up the wonders, sip through the maze,
Life's a carnival, in fizzy displays.

So here's to the jests, the glee in the glass,
In moments like these, how quickly they pass.
With joy and with laughter, let's raise a toast,
To the frothy dreams we cherish the most.

The Clear Canvas of Dreams

Drips of color on a canvas bright,
Splashes of laughter, oh what a sight!
The palette dances with glittered glee,
A masterpiece made for you and me.

Silly strokes, as a toddler might paint,
Creating worlds where no one could chaint.
Jellybean creatures in marshmallow skies,
Unicorns prancing with googly eyes.

A paintbrush giggles, spreading cheer wide,
As flowers bloom in purple and pride.
In this playground of whimsy and charm,
Every stroke whispers, "Come, feel the warm!"

With each playful splash, laughter takes flight,
Dreams come alive in colors so bright.
Join the fun on this canvas so free,
To find all the wonders that wait just for thee.

Forgotten Whirlwinds

Whirling leaves in a breeze so spry,
Chasing the sun with a wink and a sigh.
Spinning like dancers in gusty delight,
Tickling each other, taking flight.

In crazy circles, they whirl and they spin,
Life's such a game, let the fun begin!
With jumps and tumbles, they frolic away,
Dancing with breezes, in a breezy ballet.

What secrets they hold as they flutter by,
On the spin of a laugh, they soar and they fly.
Each twist and turn, a giggle, a shout,
In this whirly dance, there's never a doubt.

So catch the wave of this merry tour,
The world spins with cheer, that's for sure!
With playful delight, let's jump into the fun,
Join the dance of the leaves, let the laughter run.

Silhouettes in Soft Currents

In twilight's glow, shadows come alive,
Twisting and turning, they giggle and dive.
Rippling waters, they splash and they play,
Creating a ballet in twilight's array.

Oh, look at the hues, a canvas of fun,
In every soft current, the jokes have begun.
Fish with a wink, and frogs dressed in style,
At this charming soiree, life's a goofy smile.

Boats ride the waves like dreams on a spree,
Sailing through giggles, so wild and so free.
With shadows a-dancing, let's join in the spree,
In this playful realm, there's magic for thee.

So wave to the dusk, and twirl in delight,
Where silhouettes dance in the softening light.
Wave on, dear friend, let laughter ensue,
In the warm currents, just me and you.

The Fragile Symphony

In a bath of shiny dreams, they float,
Each one a giggling, plastic boat.
With a pop and a fizz, they dance so free,
Hoping no cat will claim their spree.

Laughter echoed with every gleam,
They jiggled, they wobbled, in gleeful team.
A symphony played on a soapy stage,
As tiny hands tried to catch their rage.

A parental eye, oh what a scene,
Splashing and laughing, but never mean.
Each plop and each drop, a story to tell,
Of joy in a bowl, where giggles dwell.

So here they linger, shimmering bright,
Creating a mess with pure delight.
In the heart of the fun, they twist and sway,
As childhood magic never fades away.

A World Within the Sphere

Caught in a swirl, colors collide,
Chasing reflections they cannot divide.
Inside a round world, where giggles abound,
Every bump and bounce, a laugh is found.

Little hands reach for the shiny orbs,
Creating a ruckus, while everyone swerves.
Their laughter bursts forth, a sweet, silly sound,
In a merry chase, their joy unbound.

But oh, the mishaps, the slips and the falls,
As their merry steps bounce off the walls.
With squeals of delight, they tumble and roll,
In a world full of wonder, they all lose control.

Through surfaces slick, their giggles resound,
We're all just some kids, in childhood we're drowned.
In this silly moment, floating so free,
We find our own magic, just you and me.

Glistening Horizons

On a morning bright, the sun made a show,
Little dots glimmering, all in a row.
Around every corner, each shimmer a grin,
In this joyous chase, we all just dive in.

With beaming delight, we wander and roam,
A field made of sparkle, we call it our home.
Jumping through laughter, each giggle a thrill,
As moments of joy, we continue to fill.

The air is alive with our childlike glee,
Crafting a tapestry only we see.
Dances of mirth, unhindered by time,
We spin and we swirl, with rhythm and rhyme.

In this playful land, where moments don't end,
The lightness of heart, it's the perfect blend.
So let us embrace, this fanciful ride,
As we fly through the glimmers, side by side!

The Mirror of Airy Flight

On wings of whimsy, we bounce in the sky,
Where laughter and freedom together can fly.
Each flicker of light, a playful delight,
As we seek out the dreams that dance in the night.

Oh, how they twirl in a whimsical waltz,
A crew made of joy, let's all raise our faults.
With a splash and a dash, our spirits take flight,
As we chase down the wonders hidden from sight.

In this frolic of air, where we giggle and blink,
Every ounce of our laughter can make our hearts sink.
We tiptoe on clouds, as silly as can be,
With a wink and a grin, we're forever carefree.

So let out a cheer, the sky's our domain,
With mirth as our guide, there's nothing to feign.
In the mirror of play, we capture delight,
In a whimsical dance, we take off in flight!

Dreams in a Crystal Veil

In a world where fish wear hats,
And cows can dance on floating mats.
Jellybeans jump with glee,
As we sip on sweetened tea.

Silly hats made of light,
Tickle the stars in the night.
Giggles hitch a ride on beams,
While everyone chases their dreams.

Glasses filled with lemonade,
Bright umbrellas in a parade.
Laughter echoes from the skies,
Where even the shyest bird flies.

A waltz with clouds, oh what fun,
Chasing shadows, we never run.
In this land of playful sights,
Magic swirls through starry nights.

The Harmony of Weightlessness

In a place where giggles float,
Elephants dance on a tiny boat.
A peacock struts, tail feathers wide,
While spoons and forks choose to glide.

Frogs in tuxedos croon a tune,
Under the watchful eye of the moon.
Lemon drops raining from above,
Filling the air with lighthearted love.

A sky of cotton candy dreams,
Where every smile is bursting at the seams.
Bouncing balloons with silly faces,
Keep the world in funny embraces.

Dancing socks with glee take flight,
Twinkling stars join the delight.
In this land where joy is free,
Nothing's quite as silly as can be.

Glistening Whispers

When the grass begins to giggle,
And the sun gives a cheeky wiggle.
Raindrops tap dance on my head,
While the moon plays peekaboo instead.

Whimsical whispers by the creek,
Tickle my thoughts, oh so unique.
Chasing shadows with a grin,
As silly stories start to spin.

Clouds puff up like cotton candy,
While shadows pull pranks that are dandy.
Butterflies don capes and dive,
In a world where jokes come alive.

A teddy bear that tells tall tales,
Of pirates sailing in the gales.
With each laugh our worries drift,
In this space of magical gift.

Translucent Dreams

In a realm where whispers gleam,
And jellyfish light up a theme.
Kites made of laughter soar high,
While penguins practice their fly.

Rainbows wearing polka dot shoes,
Dance through fields without a ruse.
Each giggle rides a summer breeze,
Tickling the trees with gentle ease.

Gummy worms race on a track,
Waving goodbye, they never look back.
Muffins sing in sweet delight,
As sprinkles twinkle in moonlight.

In this dream where fun won't cease,
Every moment is a joyful feast.
With each chuckle and playful sway,
We find the magic in our play.

The Enigmatic Dance

In a room of laughter, they twirl and glide,
With cheeks all puffed up, and arms open wide.
A sudden misstep, oh what a sight,
They tumble and roll, oh what pure delight!

Round and round, like a dizzying game,
Each giggle a spark, igniting the flame.
With a wink and a nudge, they leap to the sky,
In a world of the silly, they flutter and fly.

Lightweaver's Lament

A jester in sunlight, they twist and they fold,
Chasing the shimmer, so bright and so bold.
With a pucker and pout, they bubble with glee,
Trading whispers and winks with the leaf on the tree.

But with a sashay, the light starts to fade,
The colors all slip, like a clown's grand parade.
A twist of the wrist, and a puff with a grin,
They'll dance through the dusk, let the fun now begin!

Essence of the Tranquil Wave

A ripple of giggles, the tide comes to play,
With sloshes and splashes that cheerfully sway.
They play on the shore, with toes in the sand,
Crafting castles of joy that no storm can stand.

As waves tease and laugh, they join in the fun,
A game of tag played 'neath the warm, shining sun.
With each little splash, a chorus of cheer,
Throwing worries aside, for silliness here.

Reverberations of an Illusion

In a carnival mirror, what do we see?
An elephant dancer and a clown sipping tea.
With noses as big as their hearts are round,
They spin through the fun where joy can be found.

With giggles that bounce like balloons gone astray,
They float through the air in a whimsical way.
Each twist of the frame brings a laugh to the land,
In this curious world, hand in hand we stand.

A Tidal Serenade

A sea of giggles swells and rolls,
Each wave a laugh that gently strolls.
Tiny drops dance with a splash,
Making moons in the sun's warm flash.

Floating critters wear silly hats,
Jellyfish jiggle as the tide chats.
Sandcastles scream with crooked pride,
As seashells chuckle by the shoreline wide.

The seagulls squawk a comic tune,
While crabs do the cha-cha by the dune.
Even the starfish seems to grin,
Waving at the tide as they begin.

As surf and whimsy twist and twine,
Nature's carnival will always shine.
With every splash, a joke unfurled,
In this watery, laughing world.

Glazed Horizons

On the rim of the world, a prankster dawn,
Spills syrupy colors on the lawn.
A rainbow smiles from ear to ear,
While puddles ponder just how to cheer.

Clouds fluff up in candy floss,
Twirling and twinkling, never at a loss.
Kites sail high with giggling strings,
As the sun plays tag with colorful flings.

Every glimmer rocks a frown,
Painting hues of silly clowns.
A world that spins in playful glee,
As starlight dips in a bubbly sea.

With every laugh, horizons stretch,
In this silly landscape, feelings fetch.
Let the skies crack jokes anew,
For joy's the paint, and we're the hue.

Shiny Portents

In the realm of sparkles, whispers tease,
Mirrors chuckle with the greatest ease.
Reflections twirl like a quirky dance,
Every shimmer gives a cheeky glance.

Glittering whispers fill the air,
Polished stones giggle without a care.
The moon throws winks, oh what a sight,
As raindrops giggle through the night.

Glasses clink in a cheerful trap,
While the stars invite you for a nap.
Each twinkle tells a riddle bright,
Sweet laughter wraps around the night.

A world that dazzles, what a show,
Shiny clues hiding in the flow.
Join the fun where the glinting quarrel,
For life's a laugh, and we're the carol.

Fantasies in Motion

Whimsical critters prance and hop,
In a whirlwind of dreams that never stop.
Flying high on twinkling wings,
They giggle at all the silly things.

Chasing echoes on a merry breeze,
Floating wishes ride with playful ease.
Silly shadows race in line,
Each turn a jolt of cartoon brine.

Time's a jester in this playful scene,
Stretches and shrinks, like a dancing bean.
As laughter bubbles from every nook,
The merry tale spins with each look.

Life's a carnival, so let's partake,
Join the fun, for laughter's sake.
In this magic, let us delight,
As fantasies dance into the night.

Breath of Liquid Laughter

In a frothy sea of giggles,
Silly smiles collide and drift.
Chasing whims like feather tickles,
Each soft pop—a joyous gift.

Laughter dances with the gleam,
As the waves of joy cascade.
Wobbly rounders share a dream,
In this circus, jokes parade.

Swirling glee in every twist,
Look, a bubble wearing shoes!
Floating free, as if to insist,
That all should join this playful muse.

Chuckle in the glimmer's skin,
As it teeters on a wink.
With a splash, the fun begins,
Silly thoughts just stop to think.

Perpetual Floating Memories

Moments glisten, rise and burst,
A riot of colors, bright and bold.
Each one whispers, "Oh, the thirst—"
For laughter shared, stories told.

In the air, they roll and spin,
Like silly hats caught in a breeze.
Round and round, let chaos in,
As the giggles play with ease.

Past and present, in a whirl,
Jokes and jests entwined like lace.
With every dip, we flip and twirl,
Finding joy in this wild race.

Time will bounce and stretch the scene,
In silly echoes, we will bask.
With wide eyes, and hearts so keen,
What fun to share, what a task!

The Enchantment of Delicate Curves

A delicate curve, a twinkling cheer,
Suspended dreams on a playful read.
With whispers of laughter floating near,
Watch them jiggle, watch them lead.

Each bend a promise, a jolly tease,
A roundabout of glee galore.
They wiggle like worms in a jolly breeze,
Ready for pranks, forevermore.

Twinkle toes on a skating spree,
Swirling past with ballet grace.
With each mini jig, oh, can't you see?
The world's a stage for this funny chase.

Life's a spiral, a giggle's tune,
Twisting under sunlit rays.
Catch the shimmer of the afternoon,
Where jokes are quick, and laughter stays.

Ethereal Playfulness

A skip and a hop on a translucent wave,
Floating dreams ride high and soft.
In this land where joy's the knave,
We bounce and twirl, we giggle aloft.

Dancing lights like cheeky sprites,
Bounce along the colored haze.
Each little pop ignites delights,
In a scramble of silly displays.

Joy spills over from the skies,
Painting faces with a splash.
Each moment sways and slyly flies,
In a whirlwind of features that clash.

Under the sun's watchful glance,
We tickle time with silly glee.
With every giggle—a bright romance,
In this world of whimsical spree.

Celestial Ripples

In a splash of color, spheres take flight,
Chasing each other with giggles and light.
They bounce off the walls, oh what a sight,
Wobbling and dancing, until they feel right.

A bubble parade, with a twist and a turn,
Floating and spinning, come watch how they churn.
They plop with a pop, then giggles we earn,
In a world of delight, where we all laugh and learn.

Caught in the moment, they twist and they weave,
Like jolly little jesters, up high they cleave.
A spectacle brief, yet hard to believe,
As laughter erupts, we joyfully grieve.

So here's to the play, with a wink and a nudge,
In a case of delight, let's never begrudge.
With each little burst, our hearts they will fudge,
In this realm of wonder, let's always judge!

Unraveling Reflections

In narrow pools, shadows play and squirm,
Mysteries pop like an old-fashioned worm.
Quirky little mirrors, their edges confirm,
That laughter can travel, all shapes it can firm.

A glimmer of mischief, a twinkle so bright,
The surface erupts, it's a hilarious sight.
Each peak like a giggle, in daytime's delight,
Where silliness reigns, and wrong feels so right.

Whimsical waves, they burst with finesse,
Dancing on surfaces, causing a mess.
With each little ripple, they toss and they press,
Creating a ruckus, we laugh and confess.

Oh, to be silly, lost in the spree,
Where nothing feels serious, joyful and free.
Embracing the chaos, we climb a tall tree,
In the garden of laughter, come play, you and me!

Whispers of Floating Dreams

In the sky, a wobbly dome,
Filled with giggles, all alone.
They drift and bob, a silly race,
Tickling clouds with a sly embrace.

Round they swirl in a dizzy spin,
Giggling softly, a raucous din.
A playful jump, then a gleeful pop,
As the sky grins, they never stop.

Up and down, they wiggle about,
With every bounce, they laugh and shout.
Tiny jesters in a grand parade,
In the sunlight, their pranks displayed.

So come and join this frothy dance,
Where joy and chaos take a chance.
With every sigh, their laughter gleams,
In a world of whimsy, they chase dreams.

Translucent Echoes

A wink from light as they play tag,
Chasing each other, never lag.
They shimmer bright, a liquid jest,
In every twist, they seem to jest.

Round the kitchen, they zoom around,
Bouncing off walls with a joyful sound.
Kitchen sink or grassy field,
In their antics, joy is revealed.

One takes a dive, another shall leap,
Into the unknown, a secret to keep.
They laugh in silence, a playful tease,
Floating free in a teasing breeze.

A splash of humor, a giggly cheer,
Echoes of laughter, a song to hear.
In the sunlight's glow, they twirl and sway,
Filling the air with their playful display.

Dance of the Liquid Orbs

In watery worlds, they spin and twirl,
Jumping high, giving a whirl.
With each bounce, a funny face,
They giggle and wink in this splashing race.

Chasing one another, a slippery crew,
Dancing 'round like they've had a brew.
Each rotation ends with a laugh,
As they tumble off a slippery path.

Brightly colored, they bounce and glide,
In this joyous plunge, they do not hide.
With a pop and fizz, the giggles bloom,
Creating chaos in every room.

As they party in this fluid maze,
Giving the mundane a quirky craze.
In every drop, there's a chuckling sound,
A carousel of joy that knows no bounds.

Shimmering Moments in Glass

In a crystal cup, they roll and skate,
Winking at raindrops, oh, so great!
They dance with shadows, a playful show,
In mirrored moments, joy starts to flow.

Frothy tops with whimsical flair,
Cheerful giggles fill the air.
As they tumble and dance with glee,
Their mischievous antics, pure comedy.

The sunlight catches each little twist,
Sending out smiles that can't be missed.
Sudden pops and bursts of cheer,
Liquid laughter that draws you near.

With every sip, a story unfolds,
Of joyful antics, laughter bold.
In the glass, they play and tease,
Crafting moments that aim to please.

Fragments of Dawn

Tiny spheres of laughter, they float in the air,
Chasing mischievous wind, without a care.
They dance in the sunlight, a jiggly delight,
Bumping into walls, oh what a sight!

A cat pounces softly, a flick of the tail,
They giggle and wiggle, like ships in a gale.
One teeters and tumbles, what a silly show,
Splashing on the floor, putting on a glow!

Caught in a mischief, they pop with a grin,
With each little burst, they shed a soft spin.
The room fills with chuckles, a joyful parade,
As laughter erupts, joylessly conveyed!

Morning light gleams with a chuckle and twist,
Who knew such small wonders could boil with bliss?
In a world of pure giggles, come join for a run,
With dawn creeping in, the fun has begun!

The Gleaning Surface

A shimmering mirror, oh what a tease,
Catching all moments, with effortless ease.
Reflecting the silly, the goofy, the loud,
Eagerly holding all scenes of the crowd.

The puddles of laughter, they shimmer and sway,
Waiting for pranksters to jump in the play.
With each little splash, comes a chuckle or gleam,
As chaos erupts from a whimsical dream!

What silly designs, in the shimmer they make,
A wobbly logo of giggles they take.
Each ripple's a wink, from the surface so bright,
Inviting all jesters to join in the light!

Under the sun's watch, they sparkle so free,
A canvas of humor, just waiting to be.
A gleaming display of a merry old show,
Where smiles multiply, and the good times will grow!

A Gentle Cascade

Dribbles of joy in a soft little stream,
They tumble and frolic, in a whimsical dream.
A splash here and there, and a giggle that rolls,
Creating a symphony of dance in our souls.

Each droplet a wanderer, with stories to tell,
Of trips down the hill, and a slippery swell.
They shimmer and drift, the way wishes will do,
Leaving trails of laughter, with nothing to rue!

A dance of the weather, with a chuckle or two,
Inviting the fairies to join in the brew.
With a flick and a swish, what a riot of fun,
A cascade of smiles, till the day is all done!

So let us unite in this water delight,
While the gentle cascade makes everything bright.
With every soft giggle, and shimmer that gleams,
Life flows with laughter, fulfilling our dreams!

Ephemeral Gleams

Bright sparkles of whimsy, they dart in the sun,
With each tiny twinkle, a story begun.
They dance like confetti, a party of light,
Whispering secrets of joy to ignite!

A flicker of nonsense, they flit through the air,
Chasing the shadows that linger with flair.
A glimmering promise of laughter to share,
As bubbles of glee burst, a treasure laid bare!

Each moment a jewel, so playful and rare,
In the blink of an eye, they frolic with flair.
Ephemeral gleams, living out on the edge,
Bursting with cheer, they dance on the ledge!

So let's chase each sparkle, and hold them so near,
As giggles turn grand, with nothing to fear.
In the fleeting of moments, where joy reigns supreme,
We find in each shimmer, a whimsical dream!

Wisps of Illusion

In the park, a child does chase,
A shiny orb, a tiny race.
It floats away, giggles escape,
While parents roll eyes, a funny shape.

Sipping tea, clouds dance above,
And tell of stories, quite full of love.
They swirl and twist, a show of grace,
Yet fall to puddles, a foamy lace.

A rubber duck, in pools of cheer,
Waves at ducks, without a fear.
It quacks, it slips, in watery glee,
A playful splash, a sight to see.

While shadows play in playful tricks,
The world spins fast with silly flicks.
We laugh aloud, so carefree,
Chasing light, so frivolously.

Celestial Spheres

In the sky, a round delight,
Glows like cheese, in the night.
Stars giggle, winking bright,
As comets race in silly flight.

A balloon floats, sways with glee,
It lifts a hat, takes it for tea.
The hat protests, it's quite a sight,
As laughter rolls into the night.

Giggling moonbeams stretch their arms,
Chasing dreams and silly charms.
They bounce around like restless sprites,
Tickling clouds in frolic flights.

While shadows dance, they tease and tease,
With every flair, they aim to please.
Joy erupts, as the stars play,
In this vast and funny ballet.

Veils of Light

Morning dew on leaves does shine,
A fairy's wink, the sun does dine.
Dancing colors, a playful scheme,
Each droplet's giggle, a glittering dream.

Silly echoes through the trees,
As whispers float upon the breeze.
They tug at branches, laugh and sway,
In a joyful jest, they skip away.

Chasing sunlight, colors blend,
Painting smiles that never end.
They slide down rainbows, a slippery game,
Who needs a prize, when fun is the fame?

While night creeps in with soft delights,
We catch the glow of firefly lights.
They tease the dark, a twinkling fight,
Work together, in pure delight.

Transient Embrace

A wink of joy upon the lake,
Ripples laugh, for laughter's sake.
They swirl and spin, a playful dance,
In their embrace, we take a chance.

The breeze whistles, a cheeky song,
It teases trees, before moving along.
Leaves flutter down, a clumsy flight,
As squirrels giggle at their plight.

Dancing shadows in the light,
Tickle the ground, what a sight!
They somersault, in merry jest,
While giggles bounce, they never rest.

With every spark, the night ignites,
We play along, in soft moonlight.
Life's a jest, oh what a race,
In this merry, fleeting place.

A Thousand Tiny Worlds

In a droplet, a kingdom's found,
Tiny folks jump all around.
Their laughter pops like corn on a stove,
As they dance within their watery grove.

A noble sits in a soap-made chair,
His royal crown, a bubble of air.
The jester flips through the misty haze,
With giggles echoing in soapy bays.

Through the swirling of suds, they play hide and seek,
With one tiny giggle, they all start to squeak.
Under rainbows that twist and twirl,
Each spin reveals a new, tiny world.

When the sun sets, the party won't cease,
For they leap and twirl, they dance with glee.
In this shimmering, frothy parade,
Who wouldn't join in their light-hearted trade?

Light-Infused Journeys

A lantern glimmers in silly delight,
Guiding wanderers through the night.
They trip on shadows, they tumble, they fall,
Each misstep mirrored in a glowing ball.

The path glows softly with a giggly grin,
As step by step, they spin and spin.
Every glint is a wink from the stars,
"Come and play with us, no need for cars."

Through fields of twinkling and glimmering cheer,
They chase the sparkles, never a fear.
With friends all around, each pose is a joke,
As they tumble and laugh under the starlit cloak.

In the twilight's embrace, the fun never dies,
With voices that echo bright lullabies.
In this dance of light, so absurd and grand,
Join the journey, take a hand!

Spectral Sojourn

A hop on the rainbow, a jig in the mist,
In a world of color, they can't resist.
Each hue has a giggle, each shade wears a grin,
As they swirl through the fog, let the fun begin!

Chasing ripples in puddles, they leap with glee,
Creating tiny whirlwinds of vibrant spree.
The sky grins down, tickled by their play,
While shadows stretch long and dance away.

With painted smiles and glimmery shoes,
They stomp on the ground, spread laughter like news.
Every glimmering echo bounces along,
In this serenade, they sing their own song.

The serpentine lines weave tales so bright,
In this spectral game, they frolic in light.
With a wink and a nudge, they glitz and they glide,
In this sparkling sojourn, it's fun-filled and wide.

Veiled Realities

In a world of whispers, some secrets unfold,
With playful giggles, and legends retold.
Invisible curtains shimmer with glee,
As the silly sprites dance, oh look at me!

Behind every shimmer, a prank is set,
A cartoonish twist you won't forget.
The giggles erupt like popcorn might pop,
As they bounce through this veil, they laugh 'til they drop.

The shadows play tricks, they wobble and spin,
While the bright little haunts rope you in.
With jokes made of light, and laughter so vast,
In this veiled reality, hold on to the blast.

As the curtain draws back, the nonsense shines bright,
With each mischievous soul painting the night.
In this humorous play, let joy interlace,
With funny reflections, keep up with the race!

www.ingramcontent.com/pod-product-compliance
Lightning Source LLC
Chambersburg PA
CBHW070006300426
43661CB00141B/264